WAITING FOR ANYA

Based on the book by
Michael Morpurgo

Adapted for the stage by
Simon Reade

SAMUEL FRENCH

Copyright © 2023 by Michael Morpurgo and Simon Reade
Cover design by Rebecca Pitt
All Rights Reserved

WAITING FOR ANYA is fully protected under the copyright laws of the British Commonwealth, including Canada, the United States of America, and all other countries of the Copyright Union. All rights, including professional and amateur stage productions, recitation, lecturing, public reading, motion picture, radio broadcasting, television, online/digital production, and the rights of translation into foreign languages are strictly reserved.

ISBN 978-0-573-01377-5

concordtheatricals.co.uk
concordtheatricals.com

FOR AMATEUR PRODUCTION ENQUIRIES

United Kingdom and World
excluding North America
licensing@concordtheatricals.co.uk
020-7054-7298

Each title is subject to availability from Concord Theatricals, depending upon country of performance.

CAUTION: Professional and amateur producers are hereby warned that *WAITING FOR ANYA* is subject to a licensing fee. The purchase, renting, lending or use of this book does not constitute a licence to perform this title(s), which licence must be obtained from the appropriate agent prior to any performance. Performance of this title(s) without a licence is a violation of copyright law and may subject the producer and/or presenter of such performances to penalties. Both amateurs and professionals considering a production are strongly advised to apply to the appropriate agent before starting rehearsals, advertising, or booking a theatre. A licensing fee must be paid whether the title is presented for charity or gain and whether or not admission is charged.

This work is published by Samuel French, an imprint of Concord Theatricals Ltd.

The Professional Rights in this play are controlled by Berlin Associates 7 Tyers Gate, London SE1 3HX.

No one shall make any changes in this title for the purpose of production. No part of this book may be reproduced, stored in a retrieval system, scanned, uploaded, or transmitted in any form, by any means, now known or yet to be invented, including mechanical, electronic, digital, photocopying, recording, videotaping, or otherwise, without the prior written permission of the publisher. No one shall share this title, or part of this title, to any social media or file hosting websites.

The moral right of Michael Morpurgo and Simon Reade to be identified as author of this work has been asserted in accordance with Section 77 of the Copyright, Designs and Patents Act 1988.

USE OF COPYRIGHTED MUSIC

A licence issued by Concord Theatricals to perform this play does not include permission to use the incidental music specified in this publication. In the United Kingdom: Where the place of performance is already licensed by the PERFORMING RIGHT SOCIETY (PRS) a return of the music used must be made to them. If the place of performance is not so licensed then application should be made to PRS for Music (www.prsformusic.com). A separate and additional licence from PHONOGRAPHIC PERFORMANCE LTD (www.ppluk.com) may be needed whenever commercial recordings are used. Outside the United Kingdom: Please contact the appropriate music licensing authority in your territory for the rights to any incidental music.

USE OF COPYRIGHTED THIRD-PARTY MATERIALS

Licensees are solely responsible for obtaining formal written permission from copyright owners to use copyrighted third-party materials (e.g., artworks, logos) in the performance of this play and are strongly cautioned to do so. If no such permission is obtained by the licensee, then the licensee must use only original materials that the licensee owns and controls. Licensees are solely responsible and liable for clearances of all third-party copyrighted materials, and shall indemnify the copyright owners of the play(s) and their licensing agent, Concord Theatricals Ltd., against any costs, expenses, losses and liabilities arising from the use of such copyrighted third-party materials by licensees.

IMPORTANT BILLING AND CREDIT REQUIREMENTS

If you have obtained performance rights to this title, please refer to your licensing agreement for important billing and credit requirements.

WAITING FOR ANYA was commissioned by the Barn Theatre, Cirencester where it was first performed March 27th 2023. The cast was as follows:

JO LALANDE	Jack Heydon
PIERRE LALANDE	Perri Snowdon
HENRI LALANDE	Christopher Bianchi
LISE LALANDE	Andrea Johannes
SOLOMON	Yiftach Mizrahi
MADAME HORCADA	Alison Reid
WEISSMAN/LASALLE	Tom Hendryk
WILHELM	Christopher Staines

Other parts played by members of the company.

Director – Mark Leipacher
Designer – Ceci Calf
Lighting Designer – Murong Li
Music & Sound – Asaf Zohar
Wardrobe – Denise Cleal
Casting Director – Harry Blumenau
Production Manager – Harry Armytage
Stage Managers – Zoe Morgan, Ellie Carney, Grace Noble, Grace Duckerin
Producers – Laura Earwaker, Beth Geoge
Artistic Director – Iwan Lewis

CHARACTERS

<u>The Village of Lescun</u>
JO LALANDE – (teenage)
GRANDPA, HENRI LALANDE – (60s) (pronounced O*(n)*-*ree*)
MAMA, LISE LALANDE – (30s) (pronounced *Leez*)
PAPA, PIERRE LALANDE – (30s)
FATHER LASALLE – the village priest and church organist

<u>The Mountains</u>
SOLOMON HOROVITZ – (30s)
WIDOW HORCADA, ALICE – (60s) (pronounced A-*leece*)
LÉAH – (the same age as Jo) (pronounced *Lay*-*ah*)
ANYA – (the same age as Jo) (pronounced *An*-*yah*)

<u>The Germans</u>
LIEUTENANT WEISSMANN – (pronounced *Vice*-*mann*)
CORPORAL, WILHELM – (50s) (pronounced *Vill*-*helm*)
SOLDIER

The play can be performed by at least as many performers as there are characters – or a virtue can be made a of a tight-knit, multi-role-playing ensemble of around eight. NB Jo is on stage pretty much throughout.

VILLAGERS, SOLDIERS, CHILDREN, ANIMALS etc. can be played by everyone.

NB Scene numbers are for rehearsal convenience and unnecessary scene breaks should not hold up the flow of the action.

SETTING
Set in the foothills of the Pyrenees in Nazi occupied France during the Second World War.

THANKS
With thanks to: Michael Morpurgo, Iwan Lewis, Marc Berlin & Julia Wyatt at Berlin Associates, Mark Leipacher, George Turvey.

AUTHOR'S NOTE

The story is set in a small mountain village called Lescun, that I visited by chance some forty years ago. We stayed in the only small hotel in the village square. A girl came to see us as we had dinner that evening, carrying a copy of *Cheval de Guerre – War Horse –* and asked if I could sign it. It was her uncle who kept the hotel and told her an English couple had come to stay, called Morpurgo.

I signed her book. Then she invited us to lunch in her parents' farmhouse just up the road into the mountains. So we went, had paté and bread and wine and talked. Her father, who was a sheep farmer, who made wonderful sheep's cheese from the milk, told us he'd grown up in the village during the Occupation when German soldiers came to garrison the village. They came to patrol the nearby frontier into neutral Spain, because many people, especially Jewish people, hundreds of children too, were escaping over the mountains.

He told me how it was to be occupied, how some of the Germans was really kind to them, others not. He told me of an old lady in the countryside who had hidden away Jewish children in her barns thus saving them from being sent off to the concentration camps where so many were murdered.

We walked up into the mountains afterwards and happened across a shepherd milking his sheep. He had pigs and cows and horses up there. We sat and talked and tasted his cheese; they call it *Brebis*. He told us of the bears that still lived up there and how the dog kept them away from his animals.

Then we walked up to the top of the Pic d'Anie, following the route into Spain that the refugees must have taken during the Occupation. I stood with one foot in France and another in Spain, and thought how lucky I had been in my life, my country, never to be occupied, never to be terrorised.

I came down the mountain determined to write a story about this beautiful place, the people who had lived here, the Occupation.

Luckily I had an uncle, Francis Cammaerts, who had been in the French Resistance during the Occupation, had lived and fought against the Nazi occupiers. He was very helpful to me in my research. And thank goodness, when the book came out he seemed to approve.

Since then they made a film of the book, and now Simon Reade, who has adapted so many of my books for stage and screen, has written this wonderful play which captures so well the atmosphere of the book and of the village of Lescun. Go there one day. Walk up to the Pic d'Anie, taste the cheese, and stand with one foot in France and another in Spain, and thank our lucky stars!

Michael Morpurgo, March 2023

ADAPTOR'S NOTE

Michael Morpurgo's stories see the world through the eyes of a child – the erratic, immoral, incomprehensible adult world. The adults can learn from the children; they can rediscover their childlike curiosity and open-heartedness and re-gain a fresh perspective, unsullied by the childishness of compromised adulthood. But Morpurgo's child protagonists are also naïve, where the child doesn't necessarily see the whole picture. This is a story where no one is quite what they appear to be.

The play calls for the folk music of the Occitan region sung in unison, or harmonised, *a cappella*. If the actors can strum a guitar, a mandolin or play the harmonium, then so much the better. The great anthem of the region – "Se Canto" – will weave its way through, alongside the French Revolution's National Anthem, "La Marseillaise". There will also be Jewish songs sung in Yiddish or Hebrew. And the mighty keyboard works of J.S. Bach will be played on the church organ. Humanity is redeemed through the universality of its music.

The story has plenty of strong lead characters and also a spirited community who stubbornly resist their invading aggressor, all of whom can be created by the ensemble. The production will be *Gesamtkunstwerk* – literally Total Art Work, total theatre – with the whole company utilising the practical tools of design, lighting, dance, music and deploying them all to full effect simultaneously. Sheep and trees can be played and represented by the ensemble, eagles can soar in our imagination, children can be pin-pricks of light, startled eyes shining out in the darkness. The bear could be an actor in a bearskin (maybe *Lion King*-style.) They can all be imagined and created by physically dextrous and audacious performers in a bold acoustic soundscape.

The script should be treated as a blueprint for theatrical inventiveness inspired by the director's vision, stimulated by the performers' collective imagination. As Morpurgo says: "The elements of the story, the place and the people are folded into the dough of it. Leave it to rise, bake – and it will be wonderful."

Simon Reade, March 2023

"Se Canto" is the de facto anthem of the Occitan region of southern France that traverses the Pyrenees from the Mediterranean in the west to the Atlantic in the east, and also south across the Pyrenees into Basque Spain. The song is not quite as old as the hills but it does date back eight hundred years to the 14th century. It has been passed down generation to generation by all the inhabitants of that region. Its sentiment is simple but its meaning is profound, and never more so than in a time of occupation by a foreign aggressor.

1st verse

E SOUTO MA FENESTRA — OUTSIDE MY WINDOW
I A UN AUCELOUN, — THERE IS A LITTLE BIRD,
TOUTO LA NUECH CANTO, — SINGING ALL NIGHT,
CANTO SA CANSOUN. — SINGING ITS SONG –

Chorus

SE CANTO, QUE CANTO, — IF IT SINGS, LET IT SING,
CANTO PAS PER IÉU, — IT'S NOT SINGING FOR ME,
CANTO PER MA MIO — IT SINGS FOR MY LOVE
QU'ES ALUEN DE IÉU. — WHO'S FAR AWAY FROM ME.

2nd verse

A LA FOUÒNT DE NIME — AT THE FOUNTAIN OF NÎMES
I A UN AMANDIÉ — THERE IS AN ALMOND TREE
QUE FA DE FLOUR BLANCO — WHOSE FLOWERS BLOSSOM WHITE
COUME DE PAPIÉ. — AS PAPER.

Chorus

SE CANTO, QUE CANTO, — IF IT SINGS, LET IT SING,
CANTO PAS PER IÉU, — IT'S NOT SINGING FOR ME,
CANTO PER MA MIO — IT SINGS FOR MY LOVE
QU'ES ALUEN DE IÉU. — WHO'S FAR AWAY FROM ME.

3rd verse

AQUELEI MOUNTAGNO, — THOSE MOUNTAINS
QUE TANT AUTO SOUN, — THAT ARE SO HIGH
M'EMPACHON DE VÈIRE — KEEP ME FROM SEEING
MEIS AMOUR OUNTE SOUN. — WHERE MY LOVE IS GONE.

Chorus

SE CANTO, QUE CANTO, — IF IT SINGS, LET IT SING,
CANTO PAS PER IÉU, — IT'S NOT SINGING FOR ME,

CANTO PER MA MIO	**IT SINGS FOR MY LOVE**
QU'ES ALUEN DE IÉU.	**WHO'S FAR AWAY FROM ME.**

4th verse

BASSAS-VOUS MOUNTAGNO,	LIE DOWN, O MOUNTAINS!
PLANO AUSSAS-VOUS,	AND RISE UP, O PLAINS!
PER QUE POUOSQUI VÈIRE	SO I MAY SEE
MEIS AMOUR OUNTE SOUN.	WHERE MY LOVE IS GONE.

Chorus

SE CANTO, QUE CANTO,	**IF IT SINGS, LET IT SING,**
CANTO PAS PER IÉU,	**IT'S NOT SINGING FOR ME,**
CANTO PER MA MIO	**IT SINGS FOR MY LOVE**
QU'ES ALUEN DE IÉU.	**WHO'S FAR AWAY FROM ME.**

5th verse

AQUELEI MOUNTAGNO,	THOSE MOUNTAINS
TANT S'ABAISSARAN	WILL LIE DOWN SO LOW
QUE MEIS AMOURETO	THAT MY LOST LOVE
APAREISSERAN.	WILL APPEAR CLOSER.

Chorus

SE CANTO, QUE CANTO,	**IF IT SINGS, LET IT SING,**
CANTO PAS PER IÉU,	**IT'S NOT SINGING FOR ME,**
CANTO PER MA MIO	**IT SINGS FOR MY LOVE**
QU'ES ALUEN DE IÉU.	**WHO'S FAR AWAY FROM ME.**

For Iwan

PART ONE

Scene One

(Summer. The snow-capped peak of the pyramidal Pic D'Anie looms.)

(Cicadas. Thousands of bleating sheep.)

(The whole village of Lescun drive their flocks up to the flower-rich, verdant pastures. As they do so, they sing the "Se Canto".)

(This is the Transhumance, the great nomadic transfer of livestock from the winter lowlands to the summer highlands that takes place in rural mountainous regions the world over and has done since time immemorial.)

(The "Se Canto" is hummed under:)

*(**YOUNG JO** looks up to his **PAPA** and smiles in excitement and admiration. **PAPA** looks down at his son and gives fatherly, shepherdy advice:)*

PAPA. Your first taste of the Transhumance, Jo Lalande! Each time we do this, we rejuvenate our flock of sheep, revitalise our pastures, we revive our souls! One day, my son, *you* will be driving the sheep, like your father, like my father did before me.

JO. Grandpa did this once upon a time? Grandpa looks too old to drive sheep up mountains!

GRANDPA. I wasn't always old! When I was younger it was me who stayed out for the summer months, while your Papa here would be tucked up home in bed. It's only natural that we pass on the baton to our brood. It's the way of the world. And nothing will stop it.

PAPA. Nothing except war.

GRANDPA. War? There won't be another war, Pierre. We had our fill of war last time and the Germans were soundly defeated.

JO. Will there be a war, Papa?

PAPA. Not if we refuse to fight one. But the thing about grown-ups, Jo, is that sometimes they are as daft as children.

JO. I'm not daft!

PAPA. No, you're not. Which is why I'm going to teach you the ways of being a shepherd.

JO. I know all about that, Papa. I've learned it all from you.

PAPA. Remember when you're up here in the mountains with your flock, Jo, with nothing but the beating sun and the babbling brook for days on end, you need to keep yourself busy. Milking the sheep, cheese-making, for sure. It's too easy to lie-back and enjoy God's country. But beware of predators. Beware of invaders.

JO. I'm not scared of anything, Papa.

PAPA. You might not be, brave lad, but your flock needs you to stay alert. Whittle a stick, Jo. Pick berries. Look high for the eagles if you must, but DO SOMETHING! If you do nothing on a hillside in the morning sun, with the sleepy tinkle of sheep bells all about you, well, you're bound to drop off to sleep.

JO. I can tell myself the stories you've told me.

PAPA. You can!

JO. Like the story of that one-eyed giant who trapped those men in the cave with their flock – and they could only escape by hanging on, upside-down, underneath those sheep, so the giant couldn't see them.

PAPA. You've remembered the story of the Cyclops and Odysseus!

JO. I like your stories.

PAPA. It's not my story, it's Monsieur Homer's. But I like to tell it.

JO. I like it too.

PAPA. Telling stories to yourself, Jo, making up new ones, it's a good way to keep your mind busy out here on the mountainside.

JO. I'll remember that, Papa.

PAPA. But you've got to keep your eyes busy, too, Jo, keep your eyes peeled. And whatever you do, Jo, never lie down. You can sit down, I suppose, but not *lie* down.

> *(As the "Se Canto" reaches a rousing climax of its final chorus, the urgent peel of church bells ring out in alarm, village to village, across the valley.)*

> *(The **VILLAGERS** stop, stock still. Even the sheep sense something is wrong and cease their bleating. Only the cicadas drone on incessantly, eerily.)*

GRANDPA. It's war.

> *(The skies instantly darken.)*

Scene Two

(Sirens wail, trains hoot their whistles and blast steam, as **JO**, *his* **MAMA** *and* **GRANDPA** *hug* **PAPA**, *who is now in army uniform.)*

MAMA. Come home safe, my love.

GRANDPA. And bring us back a German helmet as a souvenir!

PAPA. *(To* **JO***:)* I'll see you soon, Jo. Look after everyone for me. And the sheep!

JO. I will Papa, don't you worry. I love you!

PAPA. I love you too, Jo.

GRANDPA. Bon voyage!

MAMA. Bon chance!

JO. Bon courage!

(A stirring ensemble rendition of "La Marseillaise".)

(They wave goodbye to **PAPA** *as the train pulls out.)*

Scene Three

(The bleat of sheep in the pastures of the Pyrenean foothills. The tinkle of their bells.)

*(**JO LALANDE** is now a little older, not much wiser, and he tends his flock alone.)*

JO. *(Counting sheep.)* Seventy-seven, seventy-eight... eighty-one. Or have I counted that one already? I know there are a hundred because I was up at half-past five this morning milking every single one of them. One hundred sheep! That's a lot of milk to make a lot of cheese. Just like Papa taught me.

(He sits, and resumes his counting:) Eighty-five, eighty-six, eighty... um...

Ninety, ninety-two... seventy-three... *(He yawns.)* Not a bad life, being a shepherd, out here in the warmth of the sun.

(A lark sings beautifully, high above him.)

A skylark!

(The mew of an eagle.)

And there, an eagle! What a life! The mountains; living as high in the sky as the eagles. This is my world! And when Papa comes back from the war, when we've hammered the Germans, when all the men come back home...

(He yawns.)

If only I had a stick to whittle, like Papa said. Tell yourself a story, Jo!

(He yawns again.)

I'm too tired for stories.

(He nods off.)

(The sheep bleat nervously. **JO** *doesn't hear them because he's asleep.)*

(A dark cloud passes overhead. A rumble of thunder, a whoosh of wind, the thrum of sheep taking fright, bleating in panic.)

*(***JO*** sleeps on.)*

(A grumble – a rumble – a roar!)

*(***JO*** wakes suddenly – and stands nose-to-black-snout with a creamy-brown bear.* **JO** *is mesmerised.)*

(Then the sheep go beserk.)

A bear!

*(***JO*** careers down towards the village of Lescun, arms flailing to keep his balance, legs running away with themselves, stumbling, tumbling, shouting, shrieking:)*

Bear! Bear! Bear! There's a bear come down from the mountains! A bear!

(The **VILLAGERS** *come out to see the commotion.)*

GRANDPA. You sure, Jo? You're not crying wolf?

JO. Wolf? No, Grandpa. It's not a wolf. It's a bear! A bear!

(The growl of the bear mixes with the march of jack-boots as the **VILLAGERS** *grab their rifles and head up into the hills.)*

Scene Four

(The ritualised hunting party rapidly chase after the bear in a terrifying danse macabre.)

(The bear itself looms large. Baying dogs. Shrieking animals. Blood-lust humans.)

(And the ra-ta-ta-ta-tat of machineguns and hand-grenades and fighter planes and bombs and warfare.)

(The hunting of the bear shows the threatened community rising up against an invader.)

(The hunt reaches its climax – the bear is cornered – the rifles are raised – a volley of shots and a spine-tingling howl.)

(Then a terrible silence hangs over the village. Broken by a triumphal march through the village, trumpets blast, cymbals crash.)

*(The **VILLAGERS** process the bear through the streets.)*

VILLAGER. We got her! We got her!

VILLAGER. The first bear we've shot in Lescun since the last war!

VILLAGER. Death to the bear!

VILLAGER. Death to the Germans!

*(The bloodied bearskin is unceremoniously dumped at **JO**'s feet. He is sickened by the bear's corpse and his part in bringing about her death.)*

(The clatter and clang gives way to a solemn funeral march, played on a church organ.*)

---

* A licence to produce *Waiting For Anya* does not include a performance licence for any third-party or copyrighted recordings. Licensees should create their own.

Scene Five

(Solemn organ plays.*)

(The **VILLAGERS** *gather in church to hear* **FATHER LASALLE**'s *sermon,* **JO** *the most wide-eyed.)*

FATHER LASALLE. The Mountain Bear never comes close to our people unless she has to. After hibernation, in the spring, when her bodyfat is low and she has young to feed, *then* she will dare anything to find food enough to provide for herself and for her cubs. Yet she knows of people's cruelty, of man's voracious appetite for killing, and of our greed.

Bears are neither stupid nor suicidal. This bear must have been starving to risk such an attack. We must show humility in the face danger. It may not be what God teaches us, it may not be in the Bible; but it's what *life* teaches us.

(A wireless radio crackles into life.)

---

* A licence to produce *Waiting For Anya* does not include a performance licence for any third-party or copyrighted recordings. Licensees should create their own.

Scene Six

(**GRANDPA**, **MAMA** and **JO** *huddle round the radio, listening intently.*)

RADIO. *Ici Londres! This is London! The French speaking to the French!*

And now, please listen to some personal messages:

– "Jean-Claude has a stylish moustache."

– "There is a risk of fire at the insurance broker."

– "The cat is out of the basket and the crockery is no longer in the cupboard."

>   (*Morse code bips: dot-dot-dot-dash – then the opening bars of "Beethoven's Fifth Symphony".**)

JO. Do you not think the Germans can break the code? 'Escaped cats' and 'missing china?' 'Stylish moustaches?'

GRANDPA. (*Chuckling:*) No! And they'll be furious by the taunts of V for VICTORY da-da-da-DA!

MAMA. I just want it to be over. I want your papa home, Jo. I want it like it was before.

GRANDPA. That Colonel in London – Colonel Charles de Gaulle – he's our best hope. Him and the English. True, I don't like the English, but they're fighting the Germans and, as everyone says, your enemy's enemy is your friend. I fought the Germans in the trenches in the last war –

---

* A licence to produce *Waiting For Anya* does not include a performance licence for any third-party or copyrighted music. Licensees should create an original composition or use music in the public domain. For further information, please see the Music and Third-Party Materials Use Note on page iii

JO. You told us, Grandpa.

GRANDPA. Battle of Verdun. Longest battle of the whole war. We beat the Germans before, and we'll beat them again.

JO. How do you know?

GRANDPA. I know that we must.

JO. Why?

GRANDPA. Because if we don't, there'll be nothing left for you, Jo. Nothing worth having. Nothing worth living for.

*(**GRANDPA** realises he's being maudlin.)*

What a lot of questions you ask! Now off to work with you!

(The bleat of sheep.)

Scene Seven

*(**JO** tends the sheep. A mist has descended.)*

(Away from the contented bleating of sheep, there is a plaintive whining.)

JO. If that's another bear, I'll chase it away this time!

*(**JO** searches for the source of the whine.)*

What's this?

*(There's a small cave – the whine is coming from within – **JO** gasps.)*

A bear-cub! *Her* cub. They'll kill him if they find him. They'll hunt him down and kill him, just like his mother.

(NB we don't have to see the bear-cub in the back of the dark cave – perhaps just a pair of startled, lit-up eyes.)

*(A movement behind **JO** – the bear-cub eagerly grunts and growls – **JO** abruptly turns around to see:)*

*(A bearded **MAN** in a dirty black coat, battered hat, stick in one hand, bottle brimming with milk in the other.)*

SOLOMON. Milk. For the little bear-cub. Will you hold my stick? We don't want to frighten him, do we?

*(**JO** isn't sure.)*

I saw the whole thing yesterday – you running off, the hunt. She could have got away, you know?

JO. Who?

SOLOMON. The mother bear. She led them away from her cub. Deliberate.

JO. He'll die out here on his own, won't he?

SOLOMON. Not if we don't let him.

>   (*The* **MAN** *goes into the cave, feeds the bear-cub – the sound of it guzzling – then he grabs it and emerges from the cave with the cub wrapped and hidden in his old coat.*)

JO. You going to let him go?

SOLOMON. Can't do that. He needs looking after.

JO. Who'll look after him?

>   (*The* **MAN** *shrugs.*)

Well, I can't. If I take him home, the villagers will kill him. Shepherds don't like bears.

SOLOMON. Well, I'll have to take him home, then, won't I?

JO. Who are you?

SOLOMON. You ask a lot of questions, young man! Who are *you*?

>   (**JO** *stares, doesn't respond.*)

Maybe it's better we don't know who each other is. And best if it stays that way.

>   (**JO** *stares; doesn't respond.*)

(*Urgent:*) There was no cub. You never met me. You never even saw me. None of this ever happened.

JO. What do you mean?

SOLOMON. Not a word to anyone – not your father, not your mother, not your best friend –

JO. My father's a prisoner of war.

(The **MAN** *nods.)*

I promise.

SOLOMON. I'd better get back. I don't want to lose my way in this mist. And don't watch where I go – where one goes, others can follow, if you understand my meaning.

JO. I think so.

SOLOMON. Don't blame yourself for yesterday. You had your job to do; the old mother bear had hers. You saved your sheep and she saved her cub. That's all there is to it.

*(***JO** *nods.)*

Besides, if none of this had happened, we'd never have met, would we?

JO. *(Quick as a flash:)* We haven't met.

SOLOMON. *(Laughing:)* And if we haven't met, then we can't say goodbye, can we?

(He walks away with the bear-cub wrapped in his coat, into the mist.)

*(***JO** *wonders if he's imagined the whole thing – then he sees that the* **MAN** *has left his stick behind.)*

JO. Hey, monsieur! Your stick!

*(***JO** *heads off into the mist and mizzle after the* **MAN**.*)*

(Gentle underscore of Klezmer-style music.*)

---

* A licence to produce *Waiting For Anya* does not include a performance licence for any third-party or copyrighted recordings. Licensees should create their own.

Scene Eight

(The mist rises to reveal a farmstead in the setting sun: the grunt of snuffling, snorting pigs. The buzz of honey bees in their hives.)

*(**JO** spots a haybarn. There's a shuffling from inside.)*

JO. The bear-cub?

*(**JO** approaches warily, holding the Man's stick in both hands to protect himself, just in case. He shoulders the door, heaves it open – light floods in.)*

(There, on the floor, is a child's abandoned shoe.)

One shoe? That's a bit odd.

*(Curious, **JO** bends to pick it up – then he hears quick, heavy breathing from the hayrack. He tentatively approaches. He stops. The breathing stops. He approaches again – the breathing starts again. He stops; it stops. Like grandmonther's footsteps.)*

*(Then **JO** bravely pulls down the hay: two eyes stare back at him, unblinking, petrified – not unlike the bear-cub, but they're a child's eyes.)*

Aaaaghhh!!!

*(Terrified, **JO** runs out of the barn, still clutching the **MAN**'s stick and the child's shoe, heaving the barn door shut.)*

(Catching his breath, he looks up and sees that there's a candle in the window of the farmstead.)

Who's in there?

> *(Curious, **JO** clambers up onto a small stack of logs beneath the window and peers inside:)*
>
> *(Inside, the **MAN** with the beard splashes water over his face.)*
>
> *(There is an **OLD WOMAN** knitting by the stove, shaking her head.)*

SOLOMON. Don't worry, Alice. He doesn't know who I am. Or what I am. Or where I live.

WIDOW HORCADA. Foolhardy, that's what it was.

SOLOMON. We'll be all right.

WIDOW HORCADA. You promised you'd only go out at night, and then you go for a walk in broad daylight! And what do you bring back? Berries? No. Wild thyme and mushrooms? No! An orphaned bear-cub!

SOLOMON. Well, the boy couldn't take him.

WIDOW HORCADA. The boy? What happens when he runs home and tells them all down in the village? Someone will put two-and-two together and they'll know the old widow's son-in-law is back from Paris. And they'll get suspicious.

SOLOMON. No one will recognise me. Not with this beard.

> *(He towels his face.)*

Worst thing about a beard? It never dries properly.

WIDOW HORCADA. They don't forget a face, Solomon – especially not your face. They may be country folk, but they're not stupid.

SOLOMON. The boy won't say anything.

WIDOW HORCADA. How can you be so sure?

SOLOMON. I can always tell the honest ones.

WIDOW HORCADA. What good is intuition in times like these? You're not being rational.

SOLOMON. I know I'm not all you wanted in a son-in-law, Alice, but I tell you true: you're all I could ever have wanted in a mother-in-law.

WIDOW HORCADA. *(Pushing him away:)* Go on with you!

SOLOMON. *(Holding her tight:)* I mean it. You're brave and you're good and I couldn't have done any of it without you. You know that.

WIDOW HORCADA. I don't know anything, not any more. Maybe you're right about the boy? Maybe he won't say anything – pray to God.

SOLOMON. *(Laughing:)* Your God or mine?

WIDOW HORCADA. Why not both? Just in case one of us is barking up the wrong tree.

(She reaches out and touches his face.)

You're all I've got left now Solomon, since Florence passed away.

SOLOMON. Florence was a dutiful daughter to you, a wonderful wife to me. And she would have been a strong and loving mother for little Anya. Anya knows that.

WIDOW HORCADA. If little Anya is still alive.

SOLOMON. Of course Anya is alive! How many times do I have to tell you?

WIDOW HORCADA. You've been telling me that for two months now.

SOLOMON. Two months, ten years – however long it takes, Anya will come! And when she does we will be waiting for her, just like I promised her. She knows where to come. She could walk in here tonight.

>(**WIDOW HORCADA** *looks up at the window.*)

WIDOW HORCADA. It's getting dark. I better see to the animals –

>(*She sees* **JO** *looking directly at her – he slips, an avalanche of logs!*)

(*To* **SOLOMON***:*) Hide!

>(**SOLOMON** *obeys.* **WIDOW HORCADA** *heads straight for the door, pulls it open where* **JO** *is sprawling.*)

What on earth?

>(*Scrabbling to get up, he drops both the stick and the shoe. She picks up the shoe.*)

Where did you find this, boy?

JO. In the barn – I was only looking – I brought the man's stick – I thought I heard the bear-cub –

>(**WIDOW HORCADA** *drags* **JO** *inside, fearful, furious.*)

>(**SOLOMON** *comes out of hiding.*)

SOLOMON. It's all right, it's the boy, the same boy.

WIDOW HORCADA. It's not all right. He's been in the barn. So he knows. What did you see, boy, besides the shoe?

>(**JO** *looks at his feet.*)

I don't like a child who won't look me in the eye.

>(*She reaches out and lifts* **JO***'s chin.*)

JO. I thought I saw the bear-cub. But it was a child. Like me. Wasn't it?

WIDOW HORCADA. And do you always tell the truth?

   (**JO** *thinks about it.*)

JO. Not always. But I am now, promise.

   (**WIDOW HORCADA** *smiles.*)

WIDOW HORCADA. A rare thing; an honest boy! Honest, like you said, Solomon. Boys like honey. (*To* **JO**:) You do like honey, don't you, boy?

   (**JO** *nods.*)

(*To* **SOLOMON**:) Bring the boy some bread and honey. (*To* **JO**:) Sit, boy.

   (**JO** *sits at the table.* **SOLOMON** *brings the bread and honey.*)

JO. (*To* **SOLOMON**:) The bear-cub? Have you still got him?

SOLOMON. I fed him the milk. He was strong, but hungry for more. He headed off into the mountains looking for food. There was nothing I could do.

WIDOW HORCADA. (*To* **JO**:) Eat up, eat up!

   (**JO** *guzzles the bread and honey.*)

SOLOMON. Just like a bear! Bears love honey.

WIDOW HORCADA. You're Jo Lalande.

JO. Yes.

WIDOW HORCADA. I know your father, boy. Prisoner of war, like all the young men.

JO. Yes.

WIDOW HORCADA. I knew your grandfather better though.

JO. He's not dead.

WIDOW HORCADA. I know, he's still very much alive. I nearly married him, once upon a time, young sweethearts we were. Did he ever tell you that?

JO. *(Shaking his head in wide-eyed disbelief:)* No!

WIDOW HORCADA. He had a soft spot for my honey. Ah, well, we both went our separate ways, for better or worse, for richer or poorer –

JO. *(Automatic:)* – in sickness and in health till death us do part.

WIDOW HORCADA. You're not eating, boy!

(**JO** *resumes his bread and honey.*)

You know who I am, boy, don't you?

JO. Yes. You're the Widow Horcada.

WIDOW HORCADA. The Black Widow they call me.

JO. Though not to your face.

WIDOW HORCADA. And this is Solomon, my son-in-law. Solomon Horovitz. Who you've already met.

JO. Yes.

SOLOMON. Well, I suppose you'll have to be told.

JO. Told what?

WIDOW HORCADA. As much as you need to know.

SOLOMON. What he doesn't know already – and he knows plenty – he'll have guessed at, I'm sure. And guessing is a lot more dangerous than knowing. We know we can trust him.

WIDOW HORCADA. How do we know?

SOLOMON. *(To* **JO***:)* You've not said a word to anyone, have you Jo?

(**JO** *shakes his head.*)

No. Or we'd have had the police knocking on our door, not you.

JO. I didn't knock on your door.

WIDOW HORCADA. It would have been more polite if you had.

(**SOLOMON** *sits by* **JO**.)

SOLOMON. It's difficult to know where to start, Jo. But since I'm the cause of all the trouble, I'll start with me. I am a Jew.

JO. Like in the Bible?

(**SOLOMON** *laughs.*)

SOLOMON. Yes, we're in the Bible. And there's plenty of people thinks that where we should have stayed.

(Under the following description a soundscape of jackboots and breaking glass, fire and tanks, while the lights take on a sinister hue:)

They began on their own Jews, in Germany. First they take away their work, then their property; and they make them wear yellow Stars of David stitched onto their jackets. Then they start rounding them up like sheep and send them off to the camps. We know it is happening but we think we are safe enough in Paris, me and little Anya – Anya; she's my daughter. But of course we aren't. They invade France and Paris falls. And they start rounding us Jews up as well. There is only one place left we can go: South. To Anya's grandmother.

WIDOW HORCADA. Safe as houses. If you keep out of sight. And you can be over the border in under four hours.

JO. Over the border into Spain?

SOLOMON. I walked it once. With Anya. I gave her a piggy-back most of the way.

JO. I think I met you then.

> (**ANYA** *may appear in shadow-play – in a distinctive red beret, or such-like – picking flowers.*)

You picked flowers. For my father. You and your daughter. Pinks and wild pansies. I was a toddler, too.

SOLOMON. So that was you! The shepherd's little boy! On the way up, we watched your father making cheese. On the way back, Anya picked those flowers especially for him. It's a small world!

WIDOW HORCADA. It's a cruel world.

JO. Where's Anya now?

> (*The soundscape resumes, the shadow-play – acted out as described, Anya in her distinctive beret:*)

SOLOMON. We left Paris together, Anya and me. But roads are jammed with cars and carts and people – thousands of people, everyone trying to get away, all refugees. So Anya and I make an agreement: that if we are ever separated we will find our way back here, to Grandmother's house in the hills above the village of Lescun. We will wait for each other and then we will escape together over the mountains. We said we'd wait. We promised each other.

> (*The following is terrifyingly real in strafed light and sound:*)

One evening, in the forests outside Poitiers, the planes came and machine-gun us from the air. We scatter into the trees.

When the planes have gone, I look everywhere for Anya. All through the night. And the next day; and the next. I can not find her.

(**ANYA** *has disappeared from the scene.*)

That's why I'm here. And that's why I'm staying here until Anya comes.

JO. So who is that in the haybarn?

SOLOMON. Léah. A girl from Poland. We've got more coming soon.

JO. More?

WIDOW HORCADA. Children. Jewish children. They get passed down through France and when they get here, we feed them till they're strong again.

JO. Like the bear-cub.

SOLOMON. Yes. Like the bear-cub.

WIDOW HORCADA. Strong enough for their last trek over the mountains and into Spain to safety.

JO. You help the children escape?

SOLOMON. So many of them are like Léah. She had a big family; eight brothers and sisters. When the soldiers came she was at a friend's. She comes home late and stands at a distance and stares, watching her family being taken away. She's been on the run ever since. But she got here, and that's why we will never give up hope of Anya. Because if Léah can get here all the way from Poland, then so can Anya. One day Anya will be one of those children and we will be waiting for her.

(The door handle turns and the door squeaks open on its hinges – they are all rooted to the spot.)

(A small face peers round the door.)

Léah! It's all right. Come in. Come in.

*(**LÉAH** hobbles in one shoe to the table. **JO** sees that she's staring at his unfinished bread and honey.)*

JO. Here. Eat.

*(**LÉAH** guzzles.)*

*(She sees her other shoe. **JO** gives it to her. She steps into it without looking down, without looking away from him.)*

*(**SOLOMON** sings a traditional Jewish song, in Yiddish or Hebrew*, to comfort **LÉAH**, softly at first – then his rich voice fills the space.)*

(When he has finished:)

WIDOW HORCADA. You should go home, Jo.

JO. Yes. I should.

(He gets up to leave.)

WIDOW HORCADA. And please, don't come back.

JO. Why not?

WIDOW HORCADA. You and your questions! There should be no comings and goings, or everyone will get suspicious.

JO. I understand.

---

* A licence to produce *Waiting For Anya* does not include a performance licence for any third-party or copyrighted recordings. Licensees should create their own.

WIDOW HORCADA. And if you see me in the village, don't say hello, don't even smile at me. You can stare at me – after all, you have before, haven't you?

JO. Yes, I have. Sorry.

WIDOW HORCADA. Well, I am the Black Widow, after all.

JO. Why have you told me everything you have? When it's all supposed to be a secret?

WIDOW HORCADA. Because you have kind eyes. Like your grandpa. And because secrets are lies. And because you can be trusted – Solomon was right. And one day we will *need* you to know, to have known all that you now know. Off home with you! And love to your Grandpa!

JO. What?!

WIDOW HORCADA. I'm joking, I'm joking!

(Drumming.)

Scene Nine

(Military drumming. The rumble of military vehicles. The jackboot march of troops.)

*(The **VILLAGERS** gather in the village square, including **JO**, **GRANDPA**, **MAMA**, **FATHER LASALLE**.)*

*(A **GERMAN OFFICER**, luger pistol in holster, flanked by an inscrutable older **CORPORAL**, rifle in hand, addresses the crowd:)*

LIEUTENANT WEISSMANN. My name is Lieutenant Weissmann. We have been sent here to garrison Lescun, to guard this sector. My men and I will be billeted in the priest's home by the church. We will be living among you for some time and we wish to do so as peaceably as possible. I can assure you that we will not intrude into your lives unless you compel us to.

But I am here to remind you that France is now occupied. Your village, Lescun, is a Forbidden Zone. No one goes in; and no one goes out, without proper papers which must be carried by everyone at all times. Including the children. And there are further rules that must be obeyed:

– *Eins*: there will be a strict curfew. This means that after half past nine at night no one is allowed out of their homes until their flocks need milking at dawn.

– *Zwei*: there will be round-the-clock patrols along the border.

– *Drei*: all firearms – all hunting rifles and all shotguns – must be handed in by six o'clock this evening. For everybody's safety and peace of mind.

(A thin smile.)

Bitte schön. S'il vous plaît.

We are here to guard the Frontier. There will be no further attempts to cross into Spain. You all know what will happen if you are caught helping anyone wishing to escape – prisoners of war; your so-called Resistance; Jews. To be plain, if you help them, you will be caught and you will be shot.

We want no unpleasantness but we have our job to do and we will do it.

Thank you for your attention. That is all. Heil Hitler!

> *(The **LIEUTENANT** clicks his heels and gives the Hitlergrüss. The **CORPORAL** follows suit. Then they both leave.)*

GRANDPA. What are we? Children? "Be good boys and hand in your guns!" They say their pleases and their thank yous, all very polite, but they are an occupying force and we must resist!

JO. Why do the Germans hate the Jews, Grandpa? What did they do?

GRANDPA. It's hard to say. They don't need reasons, and even if they do they invent them as they go along.

MAMA. It's time we all got back home before the curfew.

JO. *(To **GRANDPA**:)* I thought we were disobeying the rules?

GRANDPA. *Eins*: You don't disobey your mother. *Und Zwei*: you don't disobey a curfew, unless you want your head blown off.

> *(The wind rises.)*

Scene Ten

(The wind rattles the shutters.)

*(**JO** tosses and turns in bed. **JO**'s nightmare:)*

*(The bear – one of the **GERMANS** – looms large and chases **JO** out of bed and through a forest. He sees the red-bereted **ANYA**, tries to reach her.)*

*(Aeroplanes screech overhead and strafe **JO** with machinegun-fire.)*

*(He tries to reach out to **ANYA** but the branches of the trees (the people who are trees, grabbing him, his clothes) snag him, hold him back.)*

*(Then the 'trees' morph into black-helmeted soldiers who frogmarch **JO** up against a wall where they blindfold him, raise their rifles:)*

("Eins, Zwei, Drei"'- bang!)

(The shutters bang!)

*(**JO** tumbles out of bed and awakes in a frantic sweat. No soldiers. No **ANYA**.)*

*(**JO** makes a decision.)*

*(He gets dressed – lets himself out of the house quietly at dawn – and runs all the way to **WIDOW HORCADA**'s.)*

Scene Eleven

(Breathless, **JO** *raps at the door of the Farmstead.)*

*(***WIDOW HORCADA** *pulls open the door.)*

WIDOW HORCADA. You! I thought I told you to stay away?

JO. The Germans!

WIDOW HORCADA. What about the Germans?

JO. They're in Lescun; all along the Frontier. And they'll shoot anyone who tries to cross into Spain. Anyone who is a Jew!

WIDOW HORCADA. Quickly, come in, come in!

*(***JO** *goes in.* **WIDOW HORCADA** *locks the door.)*

*(***JO** *suddenly realises that* **SOLOMON** *isn't there.)*

JO. Where's Solomon?

WIDOW HORCADA. He went last night with Léah. We saw the troop movement down in the village. We feared they would come searching all the houses, all the farms. We couldn't risk the wait –

*(***SOLOMON** *hobbles in on his stick, helped by* **LÉAH.***)*

Solomon!

JO. Thank heavens!

WIDOW HORCADA. Why is Léah still here with you?

SOLOMON. *(Sitting:)* We tried to cross last night.

WIDOW HORCADA & JO. What happened?

SOLOMON. My ankle, that's what happened. It was a perfect night – lots of cloud, plenty of wind. But soldiers, soldiers everywhere.

JO. That's what I came to warn you about!

SOLOMON. I've never seen so many. That's why we ran. It must have been a rock, or a rut – I turned my ankle – you could hear it snap, like a gunshot.

WIDOW HORCADA. It's blown up like a balloon.

JO. Is it broken?

SOLOMON. It will heal, God willing. But it will take time. And when it's mended, we will try again.

JO. But the soldiers!

SOLOMON. I don't care how many soldiers they put on these mountains; we'll find a way.

WIDOW HORCADA. It's dangerous, Solomon. Even if you were fit you'd never make it over the mountains now.

SOLOMON. But there are five more of them arriving!

JO. Five more of what?

WIDOW HORCADA. Five more children to look after. And there's still more on their way.

JO. What can we do?

WIDOW HORCADA. Well, we can't send the children back where they've come from, can we? And we can't take them where they want to go. So we'll need your help.

JO. How can I help?

WIDOW HORCADA. I can't tell you, because then you would know and it wouldn't come as a surprise.

JO. What wouldn't?

WIDOW HORCADA. I'm not telling.

JO. I'm not sure I understand.

WIDOW HORCADA. You don't need to understand. Not yet. You just need to go home, like I told you before. And then you'll see.

> (**LÉAH** *starts to sing a "Polish Folk Song" – it's taken up first by* **SOLOMON**, *then by* **WIDOW HORCADA**, *then by the whole ensemble, until it reaches its uplifting climax.)*

Scene Twelve

*(Back at home, **GRANDPA** and **MAMA** are not convinced by **JO**'s excuses about his absence.)*

GRANDPA. So. You were looking for eagles' nests?

JO. Course.

GRANDPA. But eagles don't lay their eggs until the spring.

JO. *(Faltering:)* Which is why I was looking for the nests now. So I'd know where to find them. The eggs. Next spring.

MAMA. Never mind about the eagles, what about the patrols?

JO. I didn't see any.

MAMA. Did you have your papers?

JO. No.

MAMA. Oh, Jo!

JO. Well, I didn't need them, did I?

MAMA. You're growing up too fast! If only your father were here –

GRANDPA. He'll be back home soon, Lise.

MAMA. Will he? Not if this war carries on like this.

GRANDPA. He's a prisoner of war. Safest thing for a soldier to be in a war.

MAMA. The worst thing is not knowing where he is. If I knew where he was, if I could look at a map and say "that's where he is"– well, that would be something.

JO. Wherever he is, he is safe. I know he is, Mama.

*(She reaches out her hand to **JO**.)*

MAMA. Jo, Jo.

JO. I miss him.

MAMA. I miss him too.

GRANDPA. And he'll be missing the both of you.

>*(They all three hug.)*

Now come on, Jo, we've got the sheep to see to.

>*(Music.*)*

---

* A licence to produce *Waiting For Anya* does not include a performance licence for any third-party or copyrighted recordings. Licensees should create their own.

Scene Thirteen

(*Music.* **GRANDPA** and **JO** walk through the village, **GRANDPA** with his shepherd's crook.*)

GRANDPA. You know what I fancy, Jo, when we get back from the sheep?

JO. Don't tell me. Ham and eggs?

GRANDPA. I love a good slice of French ham!

(*The village shop. As **GRANDPA** and **JO** pass by, the shop doorbell tinkles and out steps **WIDOW HORCADA** with two heavily-laden baskets of food shopping.*)

Alice! You're looking younger than ever!

WIDOW HORCADA. Go on with you, you old goat!

(*He kisses her warmly on both cheeks. She pushes him away.*)

Henri! –

JO. (*Mouthing to himself:*) 'Henri'?

WIDOW HORCADA. (*To **GRANDPA**:*) What will people think?

GRANDPA. Let them think what they like! I'm too old to care and so are you.

(*At this moment, the **CORPORAL** and another **SOLDIER** come around the corner, carrying their rifles over their shoulders. They stop – respectfully doffing their military caps at the trio –*)

---

* A licence to produce *Waiting For Anya* does not include a performance licence for any third-party or copyrighted recordings. Licensees should create their own.

CORPORAL. Bon journée, madame, messieurs.

(And then move on, having clocked and made a mental note of this trio of two oldies and a youngster.)

GRANDPA. Hard to believe, but that old Corporal and me, we were very likely shooting at each other at Verdun.

WIDOW HORCADA. How many of them are there?

GRANDPA. A whole platoon, in this village alone. They mean business. No one's going to venture over those mountain passes ever again, not now.

WIDOW HORCADA. *(Eyeing* **JO***:)* This your grandson?

GRANDPA. *(Proudly:)* He is.

WIDOW HORCADA. Doesn't have much to say for himself, does he?

GRANDPA. *(Nudging* **JO***:)* Go on, Jo, she may look fierce but she won't bite.

JO. Bonjour, Madame.

WIDOW HORCADA. *(To* **GRANDPA***, eyeing* **JO***:)* Strong lad, is he?

GRANDPA. Course he is. *(Squeezing* **JO***'s shoulder:)* From good stock, the best.

WIDOW HORCADA. *(Nodding:)* You wouldn't like to lend him to me, would you?

GRANDPA. Lend him?

WIDOW HORCADA. Once or twice a week, say. On approval, mind.

GRANDPA. What would he do?

WIDOW HORCADA. Do? He would do my shopping for me. It's climbing these hills, Henri – down's worse than up. My old knees aren't what they were.

GRANDPA. *(Rubbing his chin:)* I don't know. It's a bit difficult at the moment, what with the sheep, and his father being away. Don't know if we can spare him.

WIDOW HORCADA. I'll pay him a kilo of honey every week. How's that? I know you like my honey, Henri.

GRANDPA. I do!

WIDOW HORCADA. It shouldn't take more than an hour or two of his time. It would help me out enormously.

GRANDPA. Well, I expect we could manage. What do you think, Jo?

(**JO** *nods, not entirely certain.*)

When would he start?

WIDOW HORCADA. Now.

GRANDPA. Now?

(*She holds out her heaviest basket.*)

WIDOW HORCADA. Well, come along boy, I won't eat you.

(**JO** *takes the basket and dutifully follows* **WIDOW HORCADA** *back up the hill.*)

GRANDPA. *(Laughing after them:)* Mind you pay him, now!

(*Fast-walking "Bach" strikes up on the organ.*[*])

---

[*] A licence to produce *Waiting For Anya* does not include a performance licence for any third-party or copyrighted music. Licensees should create an original composition or use music in the public domain. For further information, please see the Music and Third-Party Materials Use Note on page iii

Scene Fourteen

*(**FATHER LASALLE** practises "Bach" on the church organ – appreciated by **LIEUTENANT WEISSMANN**.*)*

(People in the village go about their business, carrying hay, sweeping.)

*(As all this activity goes on, **JO** traipses up and down to the village shop with the baskets, up to the farmstead again heavily laden, back down again, up again – in a cleverly choreographed sequence by the director – to avoid suspicion.)*

*(At **WIDOW HORCADA**'s farmstead, she gives **JO** a large jar of honey and a shopping list.)*

WIDOW HORCADA. Your honey, Jo. And here's the list for next time.

JO. It's a longer shopping list than last time.

WIDOW HORCADA. That's because there are eight of them now.

JO. Eight?!

(The "Bach" organ continues.*)

---

* A licence to produce *Waiting For Anya* does not include a performance licence for any third-party or copyrighted music. Licensees should create an original composition or use music in the public domain. For further information, please see the Music and Third-Party Materials Use Note on page iii

Scene Fifteen

(As **JO** *walks back into the village he walks straight into the* **CORPORAL** *outside the village shop, his rifle slung over his shoulder.)*

(The "Bach" organ abruptly stops.)

CORPORAL. Jo Lalande, isn't it?

JO. Yes, sir.

CORPORAL. *(Suspicious:)* Whenever I see you, Jo Lalande, you are carrying those baskets. You have a big family?

JO. No, just me, my mother and grandpa. My father's a prisoner of war. Your prisoner.

CORPORAL. There's enough in those baskets to feed a family of ten!

JO. It's all for Widow Horcada, Herr Korporal, the old lady up across the pastures. She lives on her own but she's storing up for the winter. Like a squirrel!

*(***JO*** forces a laugh. The* **CORPORAL** *laughs.)*

*(***JO*** seizes the moment to head off with the fully-laden baskets.)*

CORPORAL. One moment, Jo.

*(***JO*** stops in his tracks.)*

Your papers.

JO. My papers?

CORPORAL. It's the rules – in or out of the village, you have to show your papers.

JO. But I don't have them.

CORPORAL. You don't?

JO. I mean, my mother will have my papers, somewhere at home. Do you really need to see them to know I am who I am when you already know who I am?

(*The* **CORPORAL** *weighs up this young* **MAN**, *too-clever-by-half.*)

CORPORAL. You're right, Jo. Tell you what: I'll give you a hand.

(**JO** *is wrong-footed, out-witted. The* **CORPORAL** *takes a basket.*)

The Widow Horcada's, you say?

JO. Yes. But I can manage. Honestly I can.

CORPORAL. It's not far, is it?

JO. Three, maybe four kilometres. If not five. At least.

CORPORAL. Not so far. Komm.

(*They walk on. The* **CORPORAL** *hums a Bavarian folk tune. Gentle subliminal Bavarian folk music plays.**)

(*After a short while – the music continues to play under:*)

Bavaria, you know it?

(**JO** *shakes his head.*)

In Germany, in the south. It's where I live, in a village like yours, like Lescun. I'm a forester, Jo, so for me this is like home.

JO. If the Black Widow sees you, I won't get my honey.

CORPORAL. Honey? Honig?

---

* A licence to produce *Waiting For Anya* does not include a performance licence for any third-party or copyrighted recordings. Licensees should create their own.

JO. She pays me in honey.

CORPORAL. I haven't had honey since I left Bavaria! Acacia and apple blossom honey. My wife, Gretchen, she makes it – well, the bees make it, but she looks after the bees. And my children, they love it! I'm lucky if they leave me the spoon to lick! They're all girls, my children. Three of them. Can you imagine that, Jo? *(Introspective, suddenly serious:)* I never thought I'd miss them so much. One of them, Ilse, she has gone to Berlin to work the telephones.

(*The* **CORPORAL** *puts down his basket.*)

It's so heavy! I don't know about the Widow, there's enough here to feed the five thousand!

(**JO** *seizes the* **CORPORAL**'s *basket.*)

JO. Thanks, I can take them from here.

CORPORAL. One day, I must taste your honey, ja?

JO. Jawohl!

(*The* **CORPORAL** *looks up into the mountains.*)

CORPORAL. *(Laughing:)* I am like a bear!

JO. Pardon?

CORPORAL. I like honey! And I like mountains. We have bears in my mountains too, you know? And eagles. We have eagles.

JO. So do we.

CORPORAL. *(Nodding:)* I have seen them. *(Pointed:)* And vultures too. Have you ever seen eagles through binoculars, Jo?

JO. No.

*(**JO** is concerned about how much the **CORPORAL** appears to know, how much he has spied, how much of a threat he could be.)*

CORPORAL. *(Peers through his binoculars:)* With binoculars you can see an eagle as close as your nose, as if you can reach out and touch it.

*(Still looking through the binoculars, the **CORPORAL** reaches out and touches **JO** – it feels sinister.)*

In the spring – Frühling – we will go up into the mountains together; and we will look for eagles with my binoculars, ja? That's a promise.

*(**JO** nods, afraid. Whatever the **CORPORAL** says sounds sinister to **JO**.)*

Well, auf wiedersehen, mein Junge.

JO. Au revoir, Monsieur.

*(**JO** watches him go. In huge relief. He picks up the baskets and heads off to **WIDOW HORCADA**'s.)*

*(Unseen by **JO**, the **CORPORAL** stops, turns and raises his binoculars to spy where **JO** goes.)*

(Then he lowers the binoculars and takes out his notebook and makes a note.)

*(He looks up again and gives one last steely gaze in **JO**'s direction, hitches his rifle on his shoulder and departs.)*

(A loud knock at the door –)

Scene Sixteen

*(**JO** knocks at **WIDOW HORCADA**'s door.)*

JO. Knock, knock! Can I come in?

WIDOW HORCADA. Of course, Jo. We were just about to eat soup, Solomon and I. Join us.

SOLOMON. Hello, Jo.

*(**JO** joins **SOLOMON** who hobbles to the table on his stick. **WIDOW HORCADA** ladles the steaming soup.)*

Thank you, Jo.

JO. Whatever for?

SOLOMON. For everything you have done for us already.

JO. It's the least I could do for you – for Léah, for the children.

SOLOMON. We don't want to ask you for more –

JO. More what?

WIDOW HORCADA. We need money, Jo.

JO. *(Incredulous:)* I haven't got any money!

WIDOW HORCADA. No, of course not! We wouldn't dream of asking you for money. We haven't got enough money to go on buying food through the winter. There's ten of them in the barn now.

JO. Ten!

WIDOW HORCADA. I haven't even got any honey left to pay you.

JO. That's all right.

WIDOW HORCADA. But there is one thing we can do.

JO. What's that?

WIDOW HORCADA. Sell the pigs.

JO. Really?

SOLOMON. We don't eat pork, you see, us Jews, the Jewish children. With the money they'd fetch we could feed an army.

WIDOW HORCADA. But I'm not selling them to just anyone. There's only one other person knows about pigs in this valley as much as me, and that's Henri.

JO. Henri?

WIDOW HORCADA. Your grandfather.

JO. Grandpa knows about pigs?! I thought he was a shepherd?

WIDOW HORCADA. He was. Is. But as a young man he kept a herd of pigs too. He was very good at it. But his father didn't like them. Too noisy. Too ravenous.

JO. So that's why Grandpa appreciates good ham!

WIDOW HORCADA. I need you to bring him up here, Jo. To see the pigs for himself.

(*JO looks across at* **SOLOMON**.)

JO. What about Solomon?

WIDOW HORCADA. Don't you worry about Solomon, he'll keep well out of sight; same as the children. Henri won't know anything, and what he won't know can't hurt him, can it?

JO. What shall I tell him, about why you want to sell your pigs?

WIDOW HORCADA. Tell him I'm old. Tell him I can't get about like I used to. Tell him what you like, Jo, but get him here.

(*The snuffle of pigs. Then snap to:*)

Scene Seventeen

GRANDPA. What? All of them?

JO. That's what she said. She told me she's too old to go on.

GRANDPA. *(Shaking his head:)* Doesn't make sense. She's always had pigs up there. She'd never sell them, not unless she had to.

JO. Perhaps she needs the money?

GRANDPA. Well, I'd like to know what for! After all, she's only got herself to look after, hasn't she? *(Rubbing his chin:)* Still, the Germans eat a lot of pork. *(Smiling.)* And that's the first invitation I've had from Alice Horcada in almost fifty years! So I'll go!

JO. Good, I'll tell her!

GRANDPA. *(Leaning forward:)* But don't you go telling your mother, Jo. She doesn't like the Widow; and she doesn't like me liking her.

JO. Why not?

GRANDPA. Oh, you know.

JO. No I don't.

GRANDPA. There's stories about me and the old widow, from the past – none true, of course. So not a word, eh?

JO. Mum's the word!

> *(More pig grunting.* **GRANDPA** *leaves hastily.)*
>
> *(A traditional upbeat "Folk song of the Occitan" plays.* Then:)*

---

* A licence to produce *Waiting For Anya* does not include a performance licence for any third-party or copyrighted recordings. Licensees should create their own.

Scene Eighteen

*(At home, **JO** eats ham and eggs.)*

JO. I can't believe Grandpa's not here to enjoy these ham and eggs! They're his favourite. Where is he, anyway, Mama?

MAMA. Out and about, I should imagine, Jo.

JO. At his age?

(A knock at the door.)

MAMA. That'll be him now.

*(**MAMA** answers the door. It's the **CORPORAL** and a fellow **SOLDIER** – both with rifles.)*

CORPORAL. Guten morgen, madame. We are searching all the houses.

MAMA. Whatever for?

CORPORAL. Orders of Lieutenant Weissmann.

*(The **SOLDIER** searches through the house while the **CORPORAL** remains with **JO** and **MAMA**, guarding them almost, as chairs are scraped across floors, cupboards opened.)*

MAMA. We've got nothing to hide!

CORPORAL. I hope you've haven't, Madame.

*(The **SOLDIER** return, shrugs to the **CORPORAL**.)*

SOLDIER. Niemands.

CORPORAL. *(To **MAMA**.)* Nothing. Danke. Danke sehr.

*(The **CORPORAL** and **SOLDIER** make to leave.)*

JO. Are you searching all the houses?

(*The* **CORPORAL** *stops, doesn't turn.*)

CORPORAL. Yes, all of them. In the village. And in the hills. Guten tag.

(*They leave.*)

(**JO** *gives it a moment, then pushes back his chair.*)

MAMA. Where are you going?

JO. (*Swiftly leaving:*) Out!

MAMA. Careful, Jo, it's dangerous!

(**JO** *rushes towards* **WIDOW HORCADA**'s – *to a manic "Bach organ Toccata" in a terrifying minor key.**)

(*As* **JO** *turns a corner, he sees the* **GERMAN SOLDIERS** *en masse, marching swiftly towards the* **WIDOW**'s.)

JO. No! Solomon, Léah! No!

(*Blackout.*)

(*Interval.*)

---

* A licence to produce *Waiting For Anya* does not include a performance licence for any third-party or copyrighted music. Licensees should create an original composition or use music in the public domain. For further information, please see the Music and Third-Party Materials Use Note on page iii

PART TWO

Scene Nineteen

(The "Bach organ Toccata" flares up.)*

*(**JO** runs towards **WIDOW HORCADA**'s and bursts in – the music stops abruptly as he stares at the scene before him:)*

*(**WIDOW HORCADA** is sat at the table smoking a pipe. And **GRANDPA** is at the stove, doing the ironing. All very domestic, if role-reversed, and calm. Looking as if the stakes couldn't be lower. But for **JO**, the stakes couldn't be higher.)*

JO. *(Incredulous:)* Grandpa?! What on earth are you doing here?

GRANDPA. What the devil are *you* doing here, Jo?

JO. What am *I* doing here? What about *you*!

GRANDPA. The pigs.

JO. But you're ironing.

WIDOW HORCADA. What is the matter?

---

* A licence to produce *Waiting For Anya* does not include a performance licence for any third-party or copyrighted music. Licensees should create an original composition or use music in the public domain. For further information, please see the Music and Third-Party Materials Use Note on page iii

JO. They're coming!

GRANDPA. Who are?

JO. The soldiers! They're searching all the houses. They're coming this way!

>(**GRANDPA** *rushes to the window.*)

GRANDPA. You sure, Jo?

JO. Course I'm sure.

>(**GRANDPA** *quickly pulls on his coat.*)

GRANDPA. *(To* **WIDOW HORCADA***:)* You'll be all right, Alice?

WIDOW HORCADA. Of course. *(Urgent, purposeful:)* And Henri: like we planned it; if we don't come for you, you'll know the worst has happened, and you'll know what to do. No goodbyes – just go.

>(**GRANDPA** *leaves.*)

JO. Where's Grandpa going? Why has he left me here with you? What was he doing here in the first place?

WIDOW HORCADA. *(Ignoring* **JO***'s questions:)* How far away are the Germans, do you think, Jo?

JO. Two minutes, one minute – maybe less!

WIDOW HORCADA. Take this: money for the shopping.

JO. But I didn't come to do the shopping!

WIDOW HORCADA. Stay and eat.

JO. *(Confused:)* You want me to stay?

WIDOW HORCADA. Of course. You go shopping for me. But boys are always hungry, aren't they? So I'll feed you first. Let's keep it natural. You eat. I'll knit.

(**JO** *can't fathom why she now appears untroubled by the imminent arrival of the* **GERMAN SOLDIERS**. *She's actually very troubled but is rehearsing what and how she's about to perform when the* **GERMANS** *arrive.*)

JO. But what about all the children?

WIDOW HORCADA. You let me do the worrying. All you've got to do is eat. Think you can manage that?

JO. Yes, all right.

(**JO** *eats. The* **WIDOW HORCADA** *knits.*)

WIDOW HORCADA. I've knitted eleven of these jumpers now. I can hardly keep up!

JO. Does Grandpa know about Solomon? Does he know about the children?

(*She stops knitting, looks up at* **JO**.)

WIDOW HORCADA. He's no fool, you grandfather.

JO. He knows?

WIDOW HORCADA. He knows everything.

(*A sudden, terrifying loud knock at the door.*)

Come in!

(*The door swings open and* **LIEUTENANT WEISSMANN** *enters with the* **CORPORAL** *and the* **SOLDIER**, *rifles in hand.*)

LIEUTENANT WEISSMANN. Guten morgen, madame. We are carrying out searches of all the houses.

WIDOW HORCADA. And what is it, precisely, that you are searching for, may one ask?

LIEUTENANT WEISSMANN. We shan't know that, madame, until we find it, shall we?

*(He instructs the **SOLDIER** to conduct the search. The **CORPORAL** stays, very much the **LIEUTENANT**'s right-hand-man.)*

*(The **LIEUTENANT** interrogates **JO**:)*

You, young man: you live in the village, do you not?

*(**JO** nods.)*

So what are you doing up here, in the mountains?

JO. Shopping.

*(In his fear, it's all **JO** can bluster.)*

LIEUTENANT WEISSMANN. Shopping?

WIDOW HORCADA. The boy does my shopping for me. He's come up here to collect the money to pay for the goods down in the village.

*(**WEISSMANN** is suspicious. The **CORPORAL** speaks:)*

CORPORAL. It's true, Herr Oberleutnant. I myself have observed the boy with the widow's baskets. Many times.

*(He takes out his notebook and shows the **LIEUTENANT** – times, dates. **JO** is aghast.)*

LIEUTENANT WEISSMANN. *(To **WIDOW HORCADA**:)* You live here all alone, madame?

WIDOW HORCADA. Yes. My husband was killed in the last war. I am quite alone.

LIEUTENANT WEISSMANN. I am sorry, madame.

(Her blood rises.)

WIDOW HORCADA. Sorry? And what is it that you are sorry for? That your stupid wars kill our husbands and fathers? That I am alone? That you are searching my house without a warrant, and treating me like a common criminal?

LIEUTENANT WEISSMANN. *(Stiffly:)* Entschuldigung, madame. *(Shouting to the* **SOLDIER**, *off; irritably.)* Etwas?

> *(The* **SOLDIER** *reappears.)*

SOLDIER. Nein, Herr Oberleutnant. Niemands.

LIEUTENANT WEISSMANN. Nothing and nobody.

> *(To* **WIDOW HORCADA**, *clicking his heels:)* Gnädige Frau.

> *(He makes to leave with the* **CORPORAL** *and the* **SOLDIER** *– but he stops at the door:)*

Just one more question, madame.

WIDOW HORCADA. What is it now?

LIEUTENANT WEISSMANN. What do you keep in your barn?

> (**JO** *looks as if all is lost.)*

WIDOW HORCADA. My barn? What do you think I keep in my barn? Fugitives? Runaways?

LIEUTENANT WEISSMANN. Madame?

WIDOW HORCADA. Animals, mein Herr. That is what farmers keep in their barns. I kept my precious pigs in my barn until I had to sell them because of the war. Now, it's just a haybarn.

LIEUTENANT WEISSMANN. Then you won't mind if we take a look?

WIDOW HORCADA. Lieutenant, let us not play games with each other any longer. You will search my barn whether I want you to or not.

LIEUTENANT WEISSMANN. Madame, I only meant that you –

WIDOW HORCADA. *(Interrupting:)* I know what you meant, Lieutenant. Just do it. Do your worst.

LIEUTENANT WEISSMANN. Danke.

> *(He and the **CORPORAL** and the **SOLDIER** leave and make their way towards the barn.)*

> *(**JO** runs to the window.)*

> *(A "Hebrew Lament" is sung a cappella under:)*

JO. They're going in! They'll find them!

WIDOW HORCADA. Find who?

JO. Solomon! The children!

WIDOW HORCADA. No they won't.

JO. Why not?

WIDOW HORCADA. They'll find hay, and bracken, and a lot of old pigs' muck.

JO. Then where are they, the children?

WIDOW HORCADA. Come away from the window.

> *(**JO** obeys.)*

And you can give me back my money before I forget.

JO. Am I not going shopping, then?

WIDOW HORCADA. *(Smiling:)* You're a brave boy, Jo.

JO. So are you. Brave, I mean.

WIDOW HORCADA. Ah, that's because when you're old and used up like I am, there's only the grave to look forward to.

JO. You aren't frightened?

WIDOW HORCADA. Nothing seems to frighten me very much any more. We'll wait for the soldiers to go – then another half an hour, just to be sure. And then we'll go and find them.

JO. Find who?

WIDOW HORCADA. The children.

JO. Where are they?

WIDOW HORCADA. You'll find out soon enough.

(The Hebrew lament continues full-throated.)

Scene Twenty

(As the Hebrew lament continues, **WIDOW HORCADA** *and* **JO** *climb the mountain path,* **JO** *helping the* **WIDOW**.*)*

(In front of them, in the trees, a curtain of old sacks. **WIDOW HORCADA** *pulls them apart to reveal:)*

*(***GRANDPA**. *And beside him,* **SOLOMON**, *at the mouth of a cave.)*

(And beyond them, within, the eyes of a dozen children – pin-prick lights in the dark, perhaps.)

*(***LÉAH** *steps forward.)*

LÉAH. Hello, Jo.

SOLOMON. Well, Jo. What do you think? Three months we've been preparing this, your grandpa and I. We've hidden our cubs in this cave, fed them with all the food you've been bringing, and now we're ready to escape into Spain.

GRANDPA. I used to sneak up here a lot as a boy, when I was your age, Jo. My father – your *great*-grandfather, Jo, God rest his soul – he used to do a bit of smuggling over the border. Brandy mostly. Don't judge – everybody was at it in those days. This is where they stored the contraband.

JO. But the German patrols are all over the mountains! And you can't take the children, Solomon – your ankle.

GRANDPA. I can take them.

JO. You?

GRANDPA. It won't surprise you to hear that I know these mountains like the back of my hand. I know gulleys and passes and caves that no German would ever know.

WIDOW HORCADA. Jo's right, Henri. You're an old man. We should wait until Solomon's ankle has properly healed. Tell me how on earth you would ever get a dozen children across the pastures without the patrols spotting you, let alone up into the mountains? You'd never manage it on your own.

SOLOMON. *(Resigned:)* Yes. It's for the best. We must wait. Wait and pray. Our time will come.

GRANDPA. *(To* **WIDOW HORCADA***:)* You've always argued with me, Alice. Trouble is, you've always been right.

JO. Why didn't you tell me, Grandpa?

GRANDPA. Tell you what?

JO. You've been coming up to the Widow's all the time, haven't you?

GRANDPA. It was safer that you didn't know. Anyway, I could ask you the same.

JO. The same what?

GRANDPA. You never told me what you were up to either, did you?

JO. No. I suppose I didn't.

GRANDPA. There you are then. I'm proud of what you've done, Jo. And your mother would be proud too, if only she knew. And your father.

JO. Where are all these children's mothers and fathers?

GRANDPA. There's some things best not to think about, Jo.

JO. Why are the Germans hunting them down like bears, Grandpa, hunting the children?

GRANDPA. There is no sane answer to that, Jo. But it's the Germans who are the bears, waiting to pounce on the children.

SOLOMON. We will wait. Until the summer. Until my ankle is healed.

(An "Occitan folk song" pipes up.*)

---

* A licence to produce *Waiting For Anya* does not include a performance licence for any third-party or copyrighted recordings. Licensees should create their own.

Scene Twenty One

(A folk song of the Occitan with a dance.*)

(The village celebrate the new season.)

*(**JO** bends down to examine a paw print in the mud.)*

VILLAGER. What's the matter, Jo Lalande? You look like you've seen a ghost!

JO. A paw print. A bear. Look at the claw marks. Best be careful with our flock.

(The song and dance climax.)

---

* A licence to produce *Waiting For Anya* does not include a performance licence for any third-party or copyrighted recordings. Licensees should create their own.

Scene Twenty Two

(Bright sunshine. Cicadas.)

*(**JO** tends sheep.)*

*(The **CORPORAL** approaches. No rifle this time, but binoculars around his neck.)*

CORPORAL. Hello, Jo.

JO. *(Startled:)* Hello.

CORPORAL. I haven't forgotten my promise.

JO. *(Nervous:)* What promise?

CORPORAL. The eagle – the binoculars – you don't remember?

JO. I remember.

CORPORAL. So let's go and look for eagles!

JO. I can't.

CORPORAL. Why not?

JO. I have to mind the sheep. Besides –

CORPORAL. Besides?

JO. You may try to appear all friendly and harmless but you are still the enemy. I can't trust you. You have your job to do just as I have mine, and you'll do your job when it comes to it; you'll behave like the enemy when you are called upon to do so.

CORPORAL. Oh, Jo. We are not enemies, you and I. Our countries may be at war with each other, because of what my country's leaders are doing to the rest of Europe. But now the German army has been driven back out of Russia, Jo. Beaten back from North Africa, too. We shall all be free soon. Free to be Freunde.

JO. Freunde?

CORPORAL. Friends. You know I had three daughters, Jo?

JO. Had?

CORPORAL. Well now I have two. Ilse was killed in an Allied bombing raid on Berlin.

JO. I'm sorry.

CORPORAL. It is very sad. But it isn't your fault, Jo. I tell myself it isn't my fault. Not if we stop this war, stop fighting.

JO. *(Suddenly angry:)* I'm not a soldier! It's you who are a soldier, all you grown-up men. If you hadn't become soldiers then you would still have three daughters, and my father wouldn't have been a prisoner of war, and those children –

CORPORAL. *(Instantly suspicious:)* What children?

JO. *(Smart as a whip:)* All God's children.

> *(The **CORPORAL** and **JO** stare at one another, daring each other, a stand-off. Eventually:)*

(Sincere:) I'm sorry about what happened to Ilse. Truly sorry.

CORPORAL. Thank you, Jo. Thank you. You're half right. If there has to be a war, then it should be fought between soldiers, not children. Before it was *only* between soldiers, that I can understand. I do not like it, but I can understand it. At Verdun it was one soldier in one colour uniform against another soldier in another colour uniform.

JO. My grandpa fought in the Battle of Verdun. He's always telling us about it.

CORPORAL. Yes. Me against your Grandpa. Fighting each other to the death. Both men. Both soldiers. What have women and children to do with the fighting of wars?

Every day since I heard about my daughter, every day I ask myself many questions and I try to answer them.

JO. Grandpa thinks I ask too many questions.

CORPORAL. It is good to ask questions, but it is not so easy to find the answers.

JO. What do you mean?

CORPORAL. Well, for instance:

– What are we doing here, Wilhelm, I ask myself?

– Answer: I am guarding the Frontier.

– Question: Why?

– Answer: To stop people escaping.

– Question: Why do they want to escape?

– Answer: Because they are in fear of their lives.

– Question: Who are these people?

– Answer: Frenchmen who do not like us, prisoners of war, Jews.

– Question: Who is it that threatens the life of Jews?

– Answer: We do.

– Question: Why?

– Answer: There is no answer.

– Question: And when they are captured, what happens?

– Answer: Concentration camp.

– Question: And then?

– Answer: No answer –

Not because there is no answer, Jo, but because we are frightened to know the answer.

*(The **CORPORAL** wipes away a tear with the back of his hand. Then he laughs, gently.)*

You see what happens when you ask too many questions, Jo? We must smile! It is good to smile. Here. Take the binoculars, Jo. Look for eagles.

JO. Thank you.

*(**JO** takes the binoculars. Looks. But sees something else, a sharp intake of breath.)*

CORPORAL. What can you see?

JO. Soldiers.

*(The **CORPORAL** takes the binoculars and looks:)*

CORPORAL. Ach, that is just Rudi's patrol.

*(He hands the binoculars back to **JO**.)*

We call them 'The Grandfathers.' They are even older than me – as old as your grandpa, perhaps! Maybe I should go down to them and show my face? We don't want them to think we are escaping over the border and shoot us, now, do we?

*(The **CORPORAL** heads off.)*

JO. What about your binoculars, Wilhelm?

*(The **CORPORAL** continues, but turns, walking backwards.)*

CORPORAL. You keep them, Jo! I have my army ones. Those ones are my own, from home. They're yours now.

*(The **CORPORAL** turns and waves his hand above his head as he continues on his way:)*

Auf wiedersehen!

(He's gone.)

JO. Au revoir.

*(**JO** is alone. The bleating of sheep.)*

*(Is he right to trust this uneasy truce between a **GERMAN CORPORAL** and himself?)*

("Bavarian folk music" strikes up again – oom-pah-pah.*)

---

* A licence to produce *Waiting For Anya* does not include a performance licence for any third-party or copyrighted recordings. Licensees should create their own.

Scene Twenty Three

> (**JO** *arrives home.* **GRANDPA** *is on the doorstep waiting for* **JO**. *The Oom-pah-pah music stops.*)

JO. What is it, Grandpa?

GRANDPA. I've got something to show you.

JO. Is something up with the children?

> (**GRANDPA** *puts his finger to his lips to shush* **JO**, *beckons* **JO** *inside.*)

What about the milking?

GRANDPA. The sheep can wait for once, Jo. Come on.

> (*They go inside.*)

> (*A* **MAN** *stands by the window with his back to them. He turns.* **JO** *is astonished:*)

JO. Papa?

> (*He rushes to his father and they hug.*)

PAPA. Let me look at you, Jo. Boy, how you've grown!

JO. Well, you've shrunk, Papa!

MAMA. They let him out of the prison, sent him home!

PAPA. They had all of me that they wanted, used me all up.

JO. Does this mean the war is over?

PAPA. No, Jo. The war is still far from over.

MAMA. Papa is sick, Jo.

PAPA. TB. Tuberculosis. They sent me home because I couldn't work any more.

JO. Are you all right, Papa?

PAPA. What's a bit of a wheezy chest when it's a passport home? Give me a week in the hills and I'll be as right as rain!

JO. Did they treat you well, Papa, in the prison?

PAPA. Don't ask me, Jo. All I can tell you is that you learn a lot of things about yourself there that you didn't know, never wanted to know.

MAMA. Jo's stepped right into your shoes here, Pierre. He's the man about the place, aren't you Jo?

GRANDPA. And what about me, Lise? Have I sat on my backside these past four years, eh?

JO. No, Grandpa!

GRANDPA. Who took the sheep up on the summer pastures for the Transhumance? I did. Who milked the sheep when Jo was busy? I did. Who stirred the vats for the cheese? –

JO. You did, Grandpa!

GRANDPA. (*To* **PAPA**:) Yes, your old father, that's who!

PAPA. Come here, Papi!

   (**PAPA** *hugs his father.*)

GRANDPA. And now you're back, son, I can hang up my boots!

MAMA. Not yet you can't, Henri. We've got to get Pierre well first. Good food and a warm house and plenty of rest, that's what he needs.

PAPA. Don't fuss me!

GRANDPA. (*Nudging his son in the ribs:*) I've been courting, son.

   (**PAPA** *laughs.*)

MAMA. It's true! Everyone knows it.

GRANDPA. Do they? How do they know? How do you know?

MAMA. You're up and down to that old widow's house every spare moment. Talk of the village!

> (**GRANDPA** and **JO** *exchange a look of concern.*)

PAPA. What old widow?

MAMA. The Widow Horcada, the Black Widow.

PAPA. *(Laughing:)* You're not serious?

GRANDPA. Wisest woman in the parish. Never parts with a penny she doesn't have to – even pays Jo in honey, doesn't she Jo?

PAPA. *(To **JO**:)* What does she pay you for?

JO. For carrying her shopping.

PAPA. *(Chuckling:)* Well, I can see I came back just in time to stop my old father making a fool of himself.

GRANDPA. Too late for that, son. I'm a smitten man and there's nothing you nor anyone else can do about it!

> (**PAPA** *puts on his coat.*)

MAMA. Where are you going?

PAPA. Out.

MAMA. Out?

PAPA. It's what I want more than anything.

MAMA. What do you mean, Pierre?

PAPA. While I was in the prison, at first I used to hold out the hope of one day seeing you again, Lise; seeing how Jo here has grown; of being home again. *(Frowning:)* You won't believe this, but then I started to forget what you all looked like. And so I stopped looking forward to seeing you because you can't look forward to something you can't remember, can you? So what I wanted to do most when I got home was to walk the hills at night, to feel alive again, to feel free. So that's what I'm going to do. And I'm going to do it right now.

(They all look at each other anxiously.)

MAMA. But you can't, Pierre. Your chest. You'll catch a chill.

PAPA. I'll be all right.

GRANDPA. Do as your wife tells you, Pierre, it's not good for you.

PAPA. Nonsense! I won't be long.

JO. You mustn't go out, Papa.

PAPA. Not you too? And why not, little man?

JO. Because there's a curfew.

PAPA. A curfew?

GRANDPA. It's true. After half past nine. If the Germans catch you outside after half past nine –

PAPA. *(Angry:)* What? What will they do? Arrest me? Put me back in prison? Shoot me? Let them!

MAMA. Pierre!

PAPA. I have been shut up for four long, stale years and now that I'm home I am not letting anyone keep me a prisoner any longer, especially not in my own home. I'll come and go as I please!

(He opens the door, pulls up his collar and walks out into the darkness.)

GRANDPA. We await the day – and it will surely not be long now – when the rest of our sons and husbands and fathers return home. Vive la France!

> *("La Marseillaise" sung by a lone voice – then others come out of their homes to join in, defiant.)*

Scene Twenty Four

*("La Marseillaise" climaxes and the whole village strike up a drinking song on bottles and glasses and boxes, all breaking the curfew to welcome **PIERRE** back from the war.)*

*(**GRANDPA**, **MAMA** and **JO** arrive, nervous – but then they throw caution to the wind and join in whole-heartedly.)*

*(Then the **CORPORAL** arrives – the music stops. Deathly silence.)*

*(The **CORPORAL** smiles at **JO**. **JO** is mortified. **PAPA** clocks this and scatters furniture.)*

PAPA. *(To **CORPORAL**:)* Look what's crept out of the woodwork. Guten abend, Herr Korporal.

CORPORAL. Good evening, monsieur. You are recently returned I understand, a prisoner of war no longer.

PAPA. No man can make me his prisoner.

CORPORAL. And you are therefore probably not aware that there is a curfew.

VILLAGER. That's what we were all trying to tell him!

CORPORAL. I see. But in coming out to tell him, Monsieur, you are all breaking the curfew.

PAPA. *(Aggressive:)* If we're breaking the curfew, Herr Korporal, then so are you! *(Not friendly:)* Come, you must join our little party.

*(**PAPA** violently grabs some glasses, a bottle of wine.)*

GRANDPA. *(To **PAPA**:)* That's enough, Pierre. *(Trying to pull him away.)* Let's all go home.

PAPA. *(Ignoring* **GRANDPA***, to the* **CORPORAL***:)* There, some good French wine. I propose a toast: to victory!

("Beethoven's Fifth Symphony" opening chords struck up by one of the **VILLAGER***'s.* Then silence.)*

(Then the **CORPORAL** *takes a glass of wine, holds it aloft:)*

CORPORAL. I drink to peace.

(The **CORPORAL** *drains his glass.)*

Auf wiedersehen. *(To* **JO***:)* Au revoir.

(The **CORPORAL** *politely leaves.)*

*(***PAPA** *has a coughing fit – the effects of TB, blood in his handkerchief.)*

*(***MAMA** *sobs;* **GRANDPA** *comforts her.)*

PAPA. *(Menacing, to* **JO***:)* I've been seeing things I don't like, Jo.

JO. What things, Papa?

GRANDPA. *(To* **PAPA***:)* Leave him be.

PAPA. *(To* **GRANDPA***:)* You stay out of this. He's my son. You and Lise, you've done enough harm as it is.

MAMA. What harm have we done?

PAPA. Just four years I've been gone and look what you've turned him into!

JO. What do you mean, Papa? What have I turned into?

PAPA. Collaborator, that's what I mean.

---

* A licence to produce *Waiting For Anya* does not include a performance licence for any third-party or copyrighted recordings. Licensees should create their own.

(A sharp intake of breath.)

JO. *(Stunned:)* What? No!

PAPA. Don't deny it! You been fraternising with that German Corporal, haven't you?

JO. Fraternising?

PAPA. In the village? In the hills?

JO. We were bird-watching, that's all – spotting eagles!

PAPA. Damn you! Don't lie to me!

*(He thumps **JO**, sending him reeling.)*

MAMA. *(To **PAPA**:)* How could you? He's your own son!

*(She and **GRANDPA** tend to **JO**.)*

What's happened to you? What have you done? What did they do to you in that prison?

PAPA. You want to know what happened? *(Breathing hard:)* They ripped my guts out, like a sheep at the abattoir. Do you understand? They took away four years of my life. And when I come back, what do I find? The whole lousy village is playing lovey-dovey with them, and my own son making friends with the filthy Bosche. Because that's what they are. Don't you know what *they* have done?

*(**MAMA** reaches for her husband's hand; he pulls it away.)*

MAMA. Pierre, please!

GRANDPA. Let me tell you something about this boy of yours, Pierre, this 'collaborator'.

JO. Don't Grandpa, you mustn't!

GRANDPA. Yes, I must. I'll not have him thinking of you like that, nor of me, nor of any of us. This boy of yours may not look like much, doesn't make a lot of noise, he just gets on with things quietly. But I'll tell you something for nothing: single-handed, this boy has been taking Alice Horcada's supplies up and down the mountain for her. Not much in that, you might say. But do you know who it's really all been for?

JO. Grandpa, no!

GRANDPA. *(Persisting:)* There are fifteen children – Jewish children – *children*! – hiding up in the forest, waiting to be taken over the Frontier and into Spain. And Jo has been bringing them the food that's kept them alive. He's fed their hope while all this time he's kept his mouth shut. That's your 'collaborator' son. That's who he's been 'collaborating' with.

(**MAMA** *is shocked.*)

MAMA. Jo, is this true?

JO. Yes, Mama. It's true.

GRANDPA. He couldn't tell you, Lise. He couldn't tell anyone. *(To* **PAPA***:)* And you know why? Because there's a law laid down by our German friends that prohibits anyone from aiding and abetting the escape of fugitives. When caught, they'll be shot. Jo's known this all the time he's been doing it. Every day of his life your son could have been taken out and shot, stone dead.

(*The shock registers – not least with* **JO.**)

(**PAPA** *looks at* **JO.**)

PAPA. Jo, what have I done to you? What have I said?

GRANDPA. Nothing that can't be undone. Nothing that can't be unsaid.

(**PAPA** *hugs* **JO.**)

PAPA. The children: they're still up there on the mountainside?

GRANDPA. They're still there. In your grandfather's old smuggling den. Biding their time until the right moment to escape across the border into Spain.

PAPA. You're crazy, crazy! At any moment a patrol could stumble across them.

GRANDPA. We know. That's why we've been waiting.

PAPA. What have you been waiting for, a miracle?

GRANDPA. Tell us how to get them across, and we'll do it!

PAPA. *(Defeated:)* I don't know. I don't know.

*(**JO** has an idea:)*

JO. *(To **PAPA**:)* Remember you told me stories from The Odyssey, Papa, when I was a boy?

PAPA. I do. What about it?

JO. One story in particular: the story of the Cyclops – the one-eyed giant –

(The "Se Canto" is hummed, like when papa told the story at the start:)

And there were all these men in a cave with the giant waiting outside ready to kill them if they tried to escape. But there were some sheep sheltering inside the cave with the men. When the sheep came out of the cave the giant didn't see them – the men clinging onto the sheep underneath, upside-down – and they all got away, safe and sound.

PAPA. You're not suggesting we strap the children, upside-down, under our flock of sheep, are you?

(Everyone laughs nervously. The "Se Canto" continues under:)

JO. No. I'm not. But sheep need shepherds, don't they? It's been a warm spring. There'll be plenty of grass on the high pastures. By my reckoning, if you take all the sheep in the village, all together, there must be, what, two thousand sheep near enough? And the pigs. And the cattle. When the time's right – and it seems to me the time's right now – we can drive the sheep and the cattle to the high pastures. And we'll need everyone in the village to do it, won't we? The Transhumance. No one will notice a few more children shepherding, will they? And once we're up on the high pastures, they can all slip away – over the border. Spain is so close up there that you can almost spit into it.

*(They all look at **JO**.)*

Just an idea.

GRANDPA. It's genius, Jo. But we'll have to get the children all down into the village from the start, so the soldiers don't notice anything untoward along the way. How on earth will we do that?

("Bach organ music" pipes up.*)

---

* A licence to produce *Waiting For Anya* does not include a performance licence for any third-party or copyrighted music. Licensees should create an original composition or use music in the public domain. For further information, please see the Music and Third-Party Materials Use Note on page iii

Scene Twenty Five

(**FATHER LASALLE** *preaches from his pulpit to the* **VILLAGERS**, *to the* **GERMANS**. *No* **JO**. *No children.*)

FATHER LASALLE. For three months every summer, our small community loses many of the men folk into the hills to tend the flocks on the lush grass on the high pastures. Since many of the men are still away at war, this summer it falls upon the old men and the children of the village to steer the sheep up into the mountains. Tomorrow begins this great exodus in earnest – the Transhumance. And to celebrate this marriage of nature and humanity, I have invited you all here – the adult villagers who are left behind; our German occupiers; while all our children are tucked up asleep in their beds before the great endeavour they'll be embarking upon at dawn – I have asked you all here, I must confess, out of my own sheer vanity.

(They look at each other, curiosity aroused.)

Vanity, vanity saith the preacher, all is vanity! *(Hand on heart:)* For many long hours I sit alone at the organ here, in the church of Saint Eulalia the Martyr of a Roman occupation two millennia ago – I sit at the organ and I practise. I have been practising some of the greatest organ music ever written – and it was written by a German, no less: one Johann Sebastian Bach. But for a musician, practise is not enough. My music must be heard. I must perform. So tonight, to mark the eve of the great Transhumance, I will give you all a recital. And you will sit here until it is finished and then, and only then, can we all go home to bed. Amen!

(He plays "Bach"*– endlessly soaring magnificent "Bach".)

---

* A licence to produce *Waiting For Anya* does not include a performance licence for any third-party or copyrighted music. Licensees should create an original composition or use music in the public domain. For further information, please see the Music and Third-Party Materials Use Note on page iii

Scene Twenty Six

("Bach organ"* segues into a cacophony of 2,000 sheep, dozens of raucous swine, bellowing cows, braying donkeys – and **VILLAGERS**, **CHILDREN**, *all whistling and whooping, church bells ringing.)*

(A cavalcade of chaos. The Transhumance.)

(This rumpus in turn segues into a stirring chorus of "Se Canto".)

(And it's all watched with fascination by **LIEUTENANT WEISSMANN** *and the* **CORPORAL***, guns at the ready.)*

(In the midst of it all, **SOLOMON** *– collar turned up, hat low over his eyes in disguise – draws* **JO** *aside:)*

JO. *(Sotto voce:)* I didn't recognise you, Solomon!

SOLOMON. *(Sotto voce:)* So much the better. I want to thank you, Jo, and all the people of this village for all that you have done.

JO. Don't thank us. It's what anyone would do – should do.

SOLOMON. What is happening here in this little place – whether it succeeds or whether it fails – it is evidence enough, if ever it were needed, that no one will ever bury the enormous power for *good*, for *compassion* in the hearts of men and women. I only have one regret –

---

* A licence to produce *Waiting For Anya* does not include a performance licence for any third-party or copyrighted music. Licensees should create an original composition or use music in the public domain. For further information, please see the Music and Third-Party Materials Use Note on page iii

JO. What is it?

SOLOMON. That my little Anya is not here.

> *(They both look around for* **ANYA** *– more in hope than any real expectation.)*

But when she comes, I shall tell her what has happened here today. I will tell her so often so that she can tell her own children; and one day, they will tell their own children. Such things as this should not be forgotten.

> *(The* **CORPORAL** *watches – he seems to suspect what is going on. He speaks to a nervous* **PAPA***:)*

CORPORAL. A hard climb for infirm men and for young children, wouldn't you say, monsieur? And you bring the pigs too?

PAPA. They all need fattening up, Herr Korporal. That's why we head into the rich pastures of the mountains every summer.

CORPORAL. Mountains. The Transhumance. It must be the same the world over. Back at home in Bavaria, we have only cows and horses. Not pigs, or sheep. And we do not all go together – women, children – just the men, the shepherds.

PAPA. *(Too quick:)* We will part company this evening with the children. I mean each shepherd will head for their own side of the mountain and we will say goodbye. To the children. The shepherds will say goodbye to the children.

CORPORAL. *(Nodding:)* The children will be coming home later?

PAPA. Yes. They'll be home. Tonight.

CORPORAL. I wish them well, monsieur.

*(There is a sudden roar – a bear – a girl's scream – and the **SOLDIERS**' shouts cry out:)*

SOLDIERS. Achtung! Achtung!

*(A reprise of the ritualised bear hunt – **LIEUTENANT WEISSMANN** is the bear, hunting down **SOLOMON** and **LÉAH** in the terrifying danse macabre.)*

*(The **CORPORAL** just looks on, torn, helpless. The others look on in horror.)*

(Baying dogs. Shrieking animals.)

*(The hunt reaches its climax – **SOLOMON** and **LÉAH** are cornered, caught in a kind of searchlight – rifles are raised –)*

(An uncanny hush falls upon the scene.)

*(**LIEUTENANT WEISSMANN** steps forward, luger pistol drawn:)*

LIEUTENANT WEISSMANN. *(To **SOLOMON**:)* Jüden? You are Jews?

SOLOMON. We are.

*(**WEISSMANN** nods. The **CORPORAL** observes, impassive.)*

LIEUTENANT WEISSMANN. We will escort you down the mountain. You will be taken from the village to the town, to the station. You will board the train –

SOLOMON. Its destination?

LIEUTENANT WEISSMANN. That is not my concern.

*(**JO** and **MAMA** and the **VILLAGERS** all stare.)*

(To **SOLOMON***:)* These are your friends? You know them?

SOLOMON. Of course not. We know no one here. No one knows us.

> *(The* **LIEUTENANT** *and the* **CORPORAL** *and* **SOLDIERS** *lead* **SOLOMON** *and* **LÉAH** *away at gunpoint.)*
>
> *(A yearning, despairing Hebrew lament sung over:)*
>
> *(The sound of a train whistle, a blast of steam, a train pulling away and then rattling over the tracks. A steel door ominously clangs shut to the echo.)*
>
> *(A deathly silence.)*
>
> *(***GRANDPA*** emerges.)*

GRANDPA. We all did what we could. Everyone did.

JO. *(Fiercely:)* Did we though? Did we? There are hundreds of us, but just a few dozen of them. And we all just stand here – like sheep! – stand dumb, and watch them take Solomon and Léah away?

GRANDPA. The other children have got away – all of them, over the border into Spain.

JO. Not Léah!

GRANDPA. A bear came lumbering into the trees, Jo. It rose on its hind legs to smite Solomon – Léah screamed – but Solomon threw stones and the bear retreated.

JO. It was the bear-cub!

GRANDPA. It was no bear-cub, believe me.

JO. No, the bear the village shot all those years ago? It was her cub, grown up.

GRANDPA. Léah's scream brought the soldiers. They were trapped. I watched. I didn't intervene. What does that make me, Jo? You have a coward for a grandfather.

(The **CORPORAL** *re-emerges; he has been listening:)*

CORPORAL. No, old man. You are not a coward. It is we who are the cowards. Me.

JO. *(To the* **CORPORAL***:)* They will be taken to one of those camps, won't they? Why? What for? What did they do?

(The **CORPORAL** *takes a deep breath:)*

CORPORAL. I have no answers, Jo. I know no answers any more, no reasons.

JO. *(Fiercely:)* They were friends of mine! Solomon has been hiding in the mountains. And do you know why? Because he has been waiting for his daughter to come, so they could escape together into Spain. He wouldn't leave here without her. And now he has left, for ever.

CORPORAL. The little girl, she was his daughter?

JO. No, that was Léah, from Poland. His daughter is called Anya. He has been waiting for her all this time. He was so sure she would come. But she never has. She never will. Not ever.

CORPORAL. Forgive me. Forgive us all.

(It thunders. Everybody leaves. Except **JO.***)*

Scene Twenty Seven

(Rain. Grey. All washed out.)

(Everyone has left the scene, except for **JO**.*)*

(He stands, drenched, looks around the empty streets.)

(The rain stops. Silence.)

*(***JO*** stares:)*

JO. *(To himself:)* They're gone. *(Aloud.)* They've gone! The Germans have gone!

(The church bells ring.)

(Someone dashes across the stage with a tattered Tricolor, like Delacroix's Liberty Leading The People.)

(Music and joie de vivre.*)

---

* A licence to produce *Waiting For Anya* does not include a performance licence for any third-party or copyrighted recordings. Licensees should create their own.

Scene Twenty Eight

(As the celebrations fade, the bleat of sheep in the pastures of the Pyrenean foothills. The tinkle of their bells.)

*(**JO LALANDE** is now a little bit older, and much much wiser. He tends his flock alone.)*

JO. *(Counting sheep:)* Seventy-seven, seventy-eight, seventy-nine – eighty-one. Or have I counted that one already? Not a bad life, being a shepherd.

(A lark sings beautifully, high above him.)

A skylark!

*(The mew of an eagle. **JO** raises the **CORPORAL**'s binoculars to get a close look:)*

And there – an eagle! Such delicate markings on its tail feathers. What a life! This is my world!

(He yawns.)

No! No yawning. I should know that by now.

(The sheep bleat.)

Think of a story to tell:

"There was once a young boy called... Jo! And Jo should have known better than to nod off while tending his flock of sheep. After all, his father had told him often enough..."

(The sound of singing, in Hebrew, like the voice of heavenly angels.)

Am I hearing things?

*(A **YOUNG WOMAN** is silhouetted in the bright sunshine, as if in a golden halo. And she wears a distinctive red beret.)*

*(**JO** is amazed:)*

Hello? Who are you?

ANYA. Anya. I am Anya.

*(**JO** smiles.)*

JO. We've been waiting for you, Anya!

*(**GRANDPA** and **WIDOW HORCADA** arm-in-arm, **PAPA** and **MAMA** holding hands, **FATHER LASALLE** and the whole village all join **JO** to greet **ANYA**.)*

GRANDPA. Welcome, Anya.

PAPA. Bienvenue.

WIDOW HORCADA. Welcome home.

(They all embrace.)

(A rousing chorus of "Se Canto".)

(The lights fade to black.)

The End

ABOUT THE AUTHOR AND ADAPTER

Michael Morpurgo OBE is one of Britain's best loved writers for children, with sales of over 35 million copies. He has written over 150 books, has served as Children's Laureate and has won many prizes, including the Smarties Prize, the Writers Guild Award, the Whitbread Award, the Blue Peter Book Award and the Eleanor Farjeon Lifetime Achievement Award. With his wife, Clare, he is the co-founder of Farms for City Children. Michael was knighted in 2018 for services to literature and charity.

Simon Reade's adaptations include: Michael Morpurgo's *Private Peaceful* (also published by Concord Theatricals/Samuel French), *An Elephant in the Garden*, *Toro! Toro!* and *Twist of Gold*; Christopher Isherwood's *A Single Man* (also published by Concord Theatricals/Samuel French); Jane Austen's *Pride & Prejudice*; Charles Dickens' *David Copperfield*; E.M. Forster's *A Room With A View*; Penelope Lively's *Moon Tiger*; *A Pure Woman* (an adaptation of Christopher Nicholson's *Winter*); Philip Pullman's *The Scarecrow & His Servant*; Geraldine McCaughrean's *Not the End of the World*; and Lewis Carroll's *Alice's Adventures in Wonderland* (TMA Award Best Show for Young People.) With Tim Supple he co-adapted Salman Rushdie's *Midnight's Children* and Ted Hughes' *Tales from Ovid* (both RSC). He wrote *Sherlock Holmes: The Final Curtain* (Theatre Royal Bath). With Paul Greengrass he co-wrote *Epitaph for the Official Secrets Act* (RSC); and with Ian Rankin he co-wrote *Rebus: A Game Called Malice*. His screenplays include: *Private Peaceful* (Goldcrest 2012) and *Journey's End* (Lionsgate/BFI 2016).

www.ingramcontent.com/pod-product-compliance
Ingram Content Group UK Ltd.
Pitfield, Milton Keynes, MK11 3LW, UK
UKHW021840210426
5322IPUK00022B/383